MY WORLD,
MY FINGERHOLD,
MY BYGOD APPLE

# My World,
# My Fingerhold,
# My Bygod Apple

POEMS BY

## Neva V. Hacker

MID-LIST PRESS

MINNEAPOLIS

FIRST SERIES: POETRY

Mid-List Press
4324-12th Avenue South, Minneapolis, MN 55407-3218

**Library of Congress Cataloging-in-Publication Data**
Hacker, Neva Vinetta, 1936-
My world, my fingerhold, my bygod apple :
poems / by Neva V. Hacker
p.    cm.    --    (First Series: Poetry)
ISBN 0-922811-25-3
I. Title    II. Series
PS3558.A286M9    1996
811' .54--dc20    95-52070    CIP

Manufactured in the United States of America

Acknowledgments for previously published poems: *ACADV Magazine* and *Embers*, "My Story"; *Atlanta Review*, "Dying in Early Spring"; *Bottomfish*, "Confrontation"; *The Bridge* and *Live Poets Society*, "Another Good Man Gone Down"; *The Child*, 2nd ed., (Mayfield, 1984) and *What's Become of Eden: Poems of Family at Century's End* (Slapering Hol Press, 1994), "Nesting Dolls"; *Contemporary Women Poets* (Merlin Press, 1977), "40th Year"; *Denver Quarterly*, "Spring"; *Foothill Quarterly*, "Advice to a Daughter" [as "Donna"], "Coffee with Gurney Norman—His Story," "Dinner at Eight," "Dinner at Eight, Again," "Magic Show," "Renaissance," "The Day the Pressure Cooker Blew Up," "To the Man Who Taught Me"; *Ignis Fatuus Review*, "Aerodynamics"; *JOPHS*, "Stargazing"; *razzmatazz*, "Wednesday Morning—West of Palestine"; *South Coast Poetry Journal*, "Light for Deborah"; *Suburban Wilderness Press*, "Plans"; *Turning Point*, "My Story," "Plans"; *WPA*, "hard rain"; *WPA 7*, "Alison, Again"; *WPA 12*, "Speaking of Fear"; *Webster Review*, "Aerodynamics," "alison, as in dreams of dreaming."

# CONTENTS

## ANOTHER GOOD MAN GONE DOWN

Aunt Pearl has cut
holes in your riding
boots and planted
hen-and-chicken cacti
in the toes, wandering
jew in the high tops. Now
she wants petunias
on your grave.
Petunias, Uncle.

You loose-footed, easy-
laughing old rogue,
I just wish
you could see what
your home-loving, long-
loving woman
has been doing since
you've been gone
this time.

AERODYNAMICS

Maxwell says
it isn't air underneath that
holds planes up, but the slice
of wind on top—across the wings.
It has something to do with cutting
the wind and forcing it to the shape
of emptiness, into which nature
—being nature and despising
any void—pulls the heavy
body up, and it appears
as a bird.

As a bird.

PLANS

I am drawing new lines
    to define the walls of a place
    in which I can live.
My old line was a horizon: it moved
    as you moved. No matter
    if you loved
    or didn't or hurt me
    or didn't, I bent to keep you
    within my limits.

Now when you call and say,
    *Get back here to your place,*
I will say, *Sorry.* No. I will not say
    *Sorry.* I will say, *I am*
    *drawing lines. This far*
    *and this far. This far.*

RELATIVE

On a gold-rimmed porcelain plate,
she handed me a piece of her liver.

Sister, I said,
    you shouldn't do that
as she cut off her arms at the shoulder joints
and motioned with her great right toe
that I should help myself to one.

The meat was stringy and needed salt.
You'll have no need for your calfskin gloves,
    I told her,
eyeing her white thighs and delicate ankles.

Lovers are embarrassed by her presence in my bed;
when I walk, I tie her to my back

in the primitive manner;
at tea,
she hangs across my knees—an awkward load
and difficult to explain; but I can't go
anywhere without my sister.

RENAISSANCE

Leave the books on the shelf   love   we are going to lie
    by water
    and taste salt   sun
    will color our too-white
    skin   and you may kiss
    my fingers   thighs
    there   there
    and   ah yes   there
    until they warm again
    and move to your rhythm
Show me no new techniques. I don't want to learn anything.

Once   twice perhaps   many times I might as well confess
    blood to my elbows
    Phaedra-like
    I searched the guts
    of sacrificial bulls
    for symbols
    that could take your place
    sweet hunger   taste
    me   taste   salt sand hair
    I am not stratosphere nor cumuli
Hard against me   now   my sweating bull. This is not for reason.

SPRING

The ground thawed in February
enough to plow.
We planted early peas,
shivering along the rows
in wool jackets.
I couldn't meet your eyes.
It had been
that kind of winter.

For days, the sun was warm
although the wind
still had the feel of frost.
I made seed flats in tomato crates
and went to bed early,
while you read
*True Adventure.*

In March, there was no sun.
You worked on tax forms.
I brought you dinner on a tray:
peas from last June,
jam from berries we had picked together.
Wind was the only voice.
All night, all day,
snow came down like thrown salt.

I have seen peas
come up through snow
in March.
Everything has limits.
When you left,
the snow was melting,
the peas dead.

## STARGAZING (ON SOME STREET WEST OF SPRINGER)

I have signed a petition to save whales and porpoises,
aware of my time.
I am older than I can imagine, having outlasted faith.
The air is thick with the breath of cities.
All large animals are endangered.
I will not live to see the planet as desert.
There is little I can do about it.

My friends are not happy with their marriages or divorces.
Mother is crazy with age.
My children open their mouths like unfeathered sparrows:
*Feed Me. Feed me.*
I have stuffed their bellies with haddock and French bread,
still they say, *Feed me.*
I try not to look at them.

Clothes do not make me beautiful or keep me warm.
I am afraid to go into the house where children cry
and that mad old woman searches the walls for Jesus.
Friends call from porches, their eyes say *Feed me.*
I run along streets without sidewalks, tripping on hedges.
When I stop, I look through this thick air
at Mars, the desert,
Jupiter, the cold.
Hurt past understanding, sometimes,
the old words come:
*Deliver us! Deliver us!*
—my voice small against the noise of traffic.

LIGHT FOR DEBORAH

When the light goes out, check, first,
the bulb: remove old, insert new. To contemplate
the meaning of darkness as metaphor is useless. Avoid
casual sex, cocaine, and too much religion. Try
to have something solid under your feet.

If you are still without power, the circuit box is one
distribution center. Do not be intimidated by labels: push
each switch in turn—off, on, off, on—until something
happens or doesn't happen. Action of any kind is better

than inaction. Sitting in a closet with a grey metal box and
a short candle is no way to spend your life. Alcohol
should not be used in times of real darkness. When you have
tried all the circuits, go back to your living room.

Try to maintain a room in which to live.

Find light. Sit in another chair. Move to another room.
You can pretend blindness, if you must, but do remember:
radical right and radical left share
a common adjective. Look out your window.

Call friends. Are they aware of this failure?
Does anyone have light?

The theory of electricity, as it relates to you, is a matter
of production and storage, of capture and storage. Power is.

I can show you how to wrap coils of copper; how to use
needlenose pliers and soldering irons. I can teach you
the assemblyline code of Black, Brown, Red, Orange, Yellow,
Grey, Blue, Violet, Green, White (Bad Boys Rape Our Young
Girls But Violet Gives Willingly).

8

Much as I love you, this is all I know:
Change the bulb. Try the switch. Tell somebody. Complain.
Pay your debts. Try to get to work on time. An open box of
baking soda will help to absorb refrigerator odors.

If you must come home, you may come without a nightshirt
    or a toothbrush.
Do not allow anyone to bring you. You drive.

## WEDNESDAY MORNING—WEST OF PALESTINE
—for Wallace Stevens

Oranges are 89 cents a pound.
August.
The day is a beetle under a heavy thumb.
The city sweats under a heavy thumb.
I am slow with heaviness
in a faded peignoir.

Christ is buried.
What remains:
a cross, a tomb, a stone,
blood in a cup.

Vines around my window are
green as a peacock's wings.
Bread rising in bakery ovens
makes the air
thick with sweetness.
It is good.
It is what I have.

But I would walk on water, if I could,
and dream
a silent river and a pale green tree—
bland fruit without death in the seed.
Here, pigeons burn their feet on sidewalks.
Their wings are clipped.

## 40TH YEAR

There are no graduation ceremonies to attend,
no weddings.
Almost everything that blooms
has bloomed
and turned to fruit.
The trees have turned
vermillion.
As we walk,
our shoulders touch.
Frost melts under our feet.

## SIMILE

There is always the temptation to compare
apples with coathooks: a squirrel
running the high wire above city traffic with
Deborah and her frantic boogaloo
from party to night club. It almost
falls right there in the middle
where exhaust fumes are surely bad
for breathing, and isn't there somewhere else
she could get whatever it is that she is after?
We have parks and back yards and a
college campus all within tree-jumping
distance. There may be a freedom
of choice and something almost
courageous in running where rabbits
certainly wouldn't run, but from here it
looks like the whole purpose is to hear us say "Oh
Oooooh," as we stand at the crosswalk and
watch the damned squirrel slip
and grab again by just one front leg
over the wire while our crossing light
changes from green to red to green
and then to red again.

Or if I do a lot of useless running
back and forth myself, trying to see
which side of the street I ought
to stand on: whether to give her
money so that she won't go
hungry or not give her money because
she might buy drugs . . .   Deborah
is unlike the fat squirrel that leaps
from the corner light pole to disappear
safely up the trunk of a live oak,
to the sound of deep sighs and spontaneous
applause.

## TO THE MAN WHO TAUGHT ME

About cells and how
they fulfill predetermined roles
so that I can smile
or taste champagne

About Y chromosomes
and X chromosomes
and how I came to be
the blue-eyed child
of a black-eyed father

About how
some little understood
chemical combination
swimming in my liver
or pituitary, perhaps,
caused your kiss
to signal parts and glands:
get ready

What seemed once
the bare-flesh wonder of your skin
reminds me only
of those busy cells:
living, dying,
shedding off like dust.

## ALISON, AS IN DREAMS OF DREAMING

We are afraid
because the webs show up.
This morning, a sticky thread from teapot to oven door;
Now I don't want to go into the kitchen.

We have set mousetraps
under the sofa and behind the china hutch.

Mother's portrait looks like the paint is cracking—
mice don't do that.

The webs show up where we have swept.
Someone says, "Stop sweeping; it is time to dance."

I dance with Earl and call him by my father's name.
You dance with someone.

You wear silk—grey silk and diamonds.
I wear the same old black velvet

with a red chiffon scarf over my shoulder.
The walls are mirrors;
I can see his hand on my back
pulling the red
scarf into an hourglass.
You wave to us;
a silver chain swings
from your wrist.

Alison, we are afraid because the webs keep showing up.
Mice don't build them, yet it is the floor we look at,
carefully setting our feet down as we dance.

14

ALISON, AGAIN

Alison, again
we sit staring into the Haviland cups—
proper as any missionary circle.
Laughter from the pool
and hickory smoke
drift through the sliding doors of the balcony.
Across the parking lot,
a juniper sheds its seeds on asphalt.
There are no buffalo.
The hippies are gone.
Leary's crowd sells turquoise on the wharf.
We travel El Camino Real, Alison,
but nobody west of Tulsa, Oklahoma,
knows where heaven is.

Someday,
some afternoon at four, perhaps,
the Goodwill truck will haul away
what we no longer use.
My poet's dress and your red sweater
will be sold for a dime each
to someone who will wash them in hot water.
Nothing is wasted:
bone turns to lime.
Flesh of man feeds flesh
of grass, of man again.
Our unremembering blood
distilled and cold
will fall as rain on Livermore.

We have looked over our shoulders
until Dante wouldn't know what to do with us.*
Alison, can't we just drink our tea,
perhaps with a little bourbon,
when the wind sounds like a bagpipe in the juniper?
Must we lean on our elbows and stare?
There is no pattern in this residue:
tea leaves cling like tea leaves to the cup.

* In *The Inferno*, seers and those who try to see the future have their heads turned
backwards as eternal punishment.

## COFFEE WITH GURNEY—HIS STORY

Kentucky U
The girl was pregnant
she said   I dropped
all my classes
and read want ads
    assistant
    clerk
    delivery
    folder, frycook
    garage helper

Snow was a grey crust
    covered with cinders
Sky was a grey crust
    covered with coal smoke
I had a toothache
Some things not even whiskey will cure

I have seen five-foot snows and earthquakes
I have been put down let down and prayed for
I don't even start to worry
until it gets that bad.

## ON THE ANNIVERSARY OF MY DAUGHTER'S DEATH ANN SAYS COME OVER FOR DINNER THERE WILL BE FOUR OF US

As I enter the door, I see that they
have arrived before me: the uninvited
missing and dead
smile and complain, plan menus.
They fill the house with their many bodies.

Into the shimmering bubble we call
"now," the past brings recipes
for poultices and gingerbread.

The dead child I must bury again each day
pulls at my skirt, and conversation fades
to background whisperings. Your children
and my children are here in all their several
ages: Dorrie is a baby on the floor,

tugging at my stockings;
she is ten or twelve, and I am trying
to tie a ribbon in place on her dark hair; she is
late getting home; she is with that awful boy and
I don't know where they have gone.
Doris is dead.

My ex-mother-in-law cooks
ham hocks and dandelion greens.
I mix dough for pie crusts.
She wants the crusts thick as pizza. She says
my crusts are like me: thin and flavorless.
These are not silent ghosts.

They argue and complain. Your children
and my children tumble screaming out of windows.
Your ex-husband and my ex-husband are talking about us.
They are like brothers. They know
that no decree or time will free us.

*(On the Anniversary of My Daughters Death . . .)*

When you ask me a question, I let my mother answer,
while I slip away to where my daughter lies
cold as winter in this August world.
Her eyes are covered with silver.

I kneel, touching her hand. Her hair,
dark as my sister's, lies straight and
smooth on the pillow. "Doris, it is quiet
here," I comfort her.   But the baby Dorrie
pulls at my shirt and cries.

## ADVICE TO A DAUGHTER

The chestnut gelding was afraid
    of lightening
    of thunder
We were never sure
whether the sudden flash from absolute
dark to clear-sky noon
or the sound
like sky breaking
sent him into the barn

Once there
    solid poplar walls
    keeping the storm outside
he couldn't stay
but danced out
flanks trembling
and his eyes
trying to see all
directions simultaneously

Remember him    Donna
    head high
    tail high
forelegs stepping like a Tennessee walker
beautiful
as you are beautiful

AN OCCASIONAL POEM

The sky is clear except
where jets from Moffett Field
draw tic-tac-toe designs:
white on blue,
the scent of Eucalyptus and Magnolia
everywhere.
Sun on asphalt
makes a veil of heat
between us
and Calderon Avenue.
    A neighbor walks
    ghostlike in the sun,
    shimmering,
    out of proportion:
    a metaphor of the metaphysical.
You stare at eaves,
where there are old bird's nests
half-fallen,
deserted webs
and cracked paint.

CONFRONTATION

Owls choke on bones of small grey mice;
young does hang from twisted strings of cross-fence;
nothing is ready.

Lately it takes no more than a hair on my sleeve
or a broken fingernail . . .

When I scream into the night sky,
"Echo, please, echo!"
there is not even a breeze to shake the juniper.

DINNER AT EIGHT

Other diners come and go; we keep our same positions.
In Belfast, Ireland, Catholics
and Protestants trade ammunition.
A poppy farmer in Ankara
is saying his morning prayer.
There may be only air above.
The Turk has my best wishes:
May his next incarnation be a New York junkie.
In our own state,
we need a better split of loaves and fishes.
I have small faith and large wishes.

We've argued God in and out of existence.
How can we get any deeper?
It's almost nine. There is proof of nothing.
The lobster is very good here, but the steak is cheaper.

People have sat like this and talked
since the first grape juice fermented.
All sides have been presented over carafes of wine.
Whatever is, remains.
We will know for certain soon or late.
Suppose, among the mushrooms on your platter,
a black angel.

Say you have to leave before dessert, your glass half-full.
If there is nothing, it won't matter.
Otherwise, my love to Uncle Jack.
If the poppy farmer is right, you may come back
wearing a pair of ragged claws.

AFTER THE SEMINAR

I have pinned the tag with my name
and company affiliation
to the corner of my desk
calendar against that sudden
day when my mind gets left
behind—like the blue raincoat
in the airport at Denver or
the good hairbrush in the Holiday Inn.
Mother forgot
that we were her
children. She called me
Papa for three years
and couldn't be trusted
out of the house. She
could only say "Papa"
to the mailman who found her
walking in the street barefoot
and wearing a torn gown.
Any day now, I will be needing
this tag, my sprig of rosemary.
For remembrance.

## HARD RAIN

where I was born
all births
were virgin births
god gave
the lord god took away
even now
I hear the voice of Noah
thunder doom

this sky is not a Baptist sky
Zeus roars
Thetis dances
in her wine-dark home
convulsive pines bow
to a sunless east
a weathercock spins
(a dying moth)
something nameless
rises in my bones

I wish god was
a hand that I could hold

somewhere between
Olympus and Hell
the class of '95
stacks sandbags
in the rain
as water that made Ararat
an isle
falls once again

SET WITHOUT SOUND:
COMMUNITY ROOM AT THE WOMEN'S SHELTER

There is a woman swimming under water,
long strokes, and her legs are shapely,
legs of a dancer. She doesn't seem to know
where she is going, and she has been
holding her breath for a long time.

On the couch, a woman turns to stare
at the faulty television stuck on mute.
Does she want to press charges?
No. He can't help getting mad. Her face
is pale but for a darkening bruise.
Apply for welfare? File for divorce?

We have completed the Personal Profile,
Description of Abuser, and the History of Violence.
I have Observed and Noted.
This is page four. How do you picture yourself
ten years from now? Five? Next week?
She stares at the TV screen and shakes her head.

It is an old movie: Esther Williams
says "I love you" under water. Bubbles
rise from her mouth, without sound.
I always want to yell,
"Get out of there, you crazy bitch!"
But I know how it is going to end.
She can certainly hold her breath for a long time.

## DINNER AT EIGHT, AGAIN

In the eye of a tunnelled wind
we have a quorum
The wind is visible with Oldsmobiles
the dust of Sophocles
and Caesar
and last year's crocus

Safe
we share
wine and applecake
count pubic hairs
lick salt
we are like summer grapes
clustered
and too warm

Sometimes a voice
disturbs our calm
The grave is safe
it says   and the cups clatter
Many times
I have almost
stepped out
and let the wind take me

DYING IN EARLY SPRING

There are things of common beauty
here: jonquils and cherry blooms.
I wish that you would bring
something from Bombay or San Francisco.
And yourself. The familiar and dear
faces of friends are not enough.

If I must, and it seems I must, go
into that dark cave Oblivion, I think
it would be loving of you to hold
a made-in-Taiwan statue of Elvis
above me in such a way that children's
grief could not hurry my leaving.

For the silly sake of all we are and were,
sing "Gatherin' o' the Clan" loudly,
lewdly; unhush this reverent air
with scandal while I become (My world!
My friends! My children! All I know!)
the memory of a lady who made bread.

# HIDING OUT IN DAVIDSON'S FIELD

Lizard, you bluetail baby
lizard, the grass is a forest
over your head where you come running,
thinking to claim your spot for sun.

How did this mountain get here?

Call me Old Woman Mountain,
lizard. Stand up
on your hind legs like tyrannosaurus rex.
Say,
*MOVE,*
*MOUNTAIN.*
I am not nearly so immovable as you think.

Take advice from me, lizard.
It is no good skittering into the brush.
It is no good skittering
into the brush.
It is no good
skittering into the brush.
Somebody has got to learn
to ROAR.

LATE WIRE

I wanted to tell you
before you took that ride to the city
with your mascara and eyeliner
and five dollars stuffed in a leather pouch

your dope stash taped to your leg

I wanted to say
above the noise of acid rock
and late-night quarrels
and ambulance sirens winding their way
up White River Road    scaring the horses

I would have told you

I wanted so much for you to know

## THIRD PERSON, TWICE REMOVED

I
a woman somewhere
blacked her breasts
and sent her children out to eat
sour apples
took the apron
where they lay curled like puppies

left them
a black book
and a three-tailed whip
true
the children saw
miracles
earthquakes in divers places
men surrounded by hellfire

she is gone
on her carved stone
god grant that she lie still
is scrawled in pencil

II
A woman once
traded her petticoat
for Desert Rose lipstick
and silk hose
then someone gave her Levis
now nothing
fits
or matches

III
I have a letter that says,
"Congratulations!
You are a free woman!"
I am reading it,
squatting before the fire,
naked as a she-thing
in the beginning.

MAGIC SHOW

I want real rabbits coming from the hat.
When the girl gets sawed,
a scream adds authenticity.
Make it believable.

If you must talk, don't quote
from *Guinness Book of World Records*.
That someone wins a polka marathon
already has me pouring bourbon in my coffee.

And snow in Michigan has no bearing on
rainfall in Milpitas.
Consider where you are.
If God is love, we are atheists.

Smile, for godsake, in your black tuxedo.
All the dead will rise, hallelujah.
Rise up, Magician.
Nobody pays for a limp act.

Forget the frightened doves
in handkerchiefs.
Give me a rose from your sleeve
and a burning candle from your pocket.

# MY STORY

After the shoe is found to be a fit
and Cinderella dons its perfect
mate, the story only has them
riding off; it doesn't give
details of life in the castle.

Having been taught by hard experience,
I distrust hasty marriage. It was
like that for me: trapped in a
chimney corner and abused, any
would-be prince looked charming.

After the ink-line drawing where she hangs
precariously across his velvet cuff
like fresh-killed game or a just-won
hunting trophy, I'd like to see
a further illustration:

The cinder lady in a royal hall, wearing
corsets and brocade and, of course, those
delicate, breakable slippers; forever
on display, she would have to walk
very, very carefully.

Having been hurt, I know how hard those
polished marble floors can be. My story
isn't really a fairytale. It does
have an obvious moral and a happy
ending: I buy my own shoes.

NESTING DOLLS

Jennifer wants
to put the baby in
the big one
first and doesn't know
what to do with
the others after
that. They fit
inside each other but
she ends up with two:
one with the baby, one
with all the rest.

Do you have any candy?
I offer her fruit
and cheese. Laura
brings me candy
Saturday, says Jennifer.
Her mother is Laura.

She calls me Mama
and she calls
her grandma Mama
and the baby sitter
Mama and the girls
her father dates
are Mama to Jennifer,
who is trying
to put a family of
nesting dolls in their places
and doesn't know
where the baby one
belongs.

## THE DAY THE PRESSURE COOKER BLEW UP

Two days of canning beans—two days!—and all we had
was 56 quarts and 7 on the stove when the men came in
and no dinner.

Then Edna Busch came by with her son
Paul, the new minister, to see why
we hadn't been in church
for two Sundays.

I hurried and slipped
a pink flowered shirtwaist dress
over my halter top
& ragged shorts
& Jacob
Russell
rumbled up
in his
red Chevrolet
3/4 ton
pickup
& yelled
that our old brindle
cow was in his
alfalfa

& the boys
went after
the cow
& the girls
went
after corn &
lettuce
for dinner
& the rest
of us sat
on the porch &
counted relatives

& nobody
was in the
kitchen
when that
half-inch-steel lid split.

## THE MORNING I GOT IT ALL TOGETHER

In the first haze of waking, before illusions
settled as certain walls, she rose. The rain
had stopped. She didn't look out the window.

Someone you love is dying, I said, as she
hurried to the kitchen, her shoes tap-tap-tapping.
I followed, trying to speak above the sound of frying.

She lifted sausages—pan to plate, pan to plate. Some
one you love is dying, I said again. She looked down
to where her feet had worn a square path:

sink to stove to refrigerator to table
to sink. She looked up to where morning
sat in the window, fresh as wet petals.

A train, on its way to somewhere,
left smoke in a thin line.
Someone you love . . .

She laughed. It was me laughing. Me
packing my bag. Me riding that train.
Clack-clack. Clack-clack.

WHITE RIVER

From the mere trickle of a stream
deep in the Boston Mountains, it pushes
forth, stubborn as a hill farmer, north,
past white oak trees and hazel nut bushes,
cutting its way through limestone,
granite, chert, splitting flint rocks
into sharp-edged, imperfect arrowheads,
gathering dirt, all the way
into Missouri, where, instead
of continuing its own contrary way,
like an aging farmer, tired,
arthritic and a bit passé,
it arches and turns southeast to run
as other rivers run, not quite as clear
but deeper in its bed.

Back when Indians camped along its banks
and brown bears fished the shoals, a white man named
Joe Coker found a valley that would grow
corn and built a mill to grind corn
for whiskey and to grind corn in exchange
for corn so that he would have corn to grind
for whiskey (which he sold for cash).
He also built a church above the mill,
safe from high water and the noisy clash
and squeak of the great water wheel.

Soon other settlers came and marked boundaries,
raised children and white corn. Their children married,
built homes. Their children's children built
houses and barns, cut timber and quarried
granite from the hillsides, sowed crops;
the place swarmed and stirred like a bee hive.
By century's end, there was a post office,
courthouse, barbershops, stores that sold
hardware and harness leather.
                              Nobody alive
remembers Joe Coker. Some remember
how the river ran, not far behind
the stores with high facades

*(White River)*

and the ruins of the old mill.
That was before Bull Shoals Dam
caused the river to swallow Lead Hill.

Sometime in the fifties, citing floods
and the need for electricity, economic gain,
more jobs, tourists, the government bought, took for
taxes, or obtained by eminent domain
town lots and river-bottom farms, made
everyone leave, cleared valley and hillside,
moved Lead Hill. It is hard to believe
that a town was ever there. Like so much hay,
the people loaded floor joists and side
meat, bureaus and canned goods, window panes,
chairs, tin roofs, fence wire. Nothing could stay.
They dug up two cemeteries and moved what was found
to high ground.

If I see catfish swimming through Mrs. Raley's
kitchen, or picture crappie minnows playing games
in the high school gymnasium, it is only imagination.
They bulldozed, from the schoolyard, cement slabs
where graduating seniors signed their names.

You can no longer see flint and limestone
shining like emeralds through 20 feet of water;
but I guess that floods occur with less
frequency, and the tourists certainly came.
The river—murky, cold, and unconcerned,
not lonely, not nostalgic, not
wondering about the folks who yearned
to stay where they had always been (the
Manleys, Milams, Raleys, Richeys, Woods:
pioneers and pilgrims, scattered and gone)
—resumes its journey to the Mississippi,
surges around and through the wonders of
hydroelectric dams and cement bridges, lifts
rich earth from the drowned gardens of old Lead Hill,
sifts it, and carries it on.

## BRINGING THE BIG ONE DOWN

Together and in love we went
to Idaho where the big
deer feed in mountain meadows, waiting
for lucky hunters and the first
day of season.
 I wish I could tell our children
that we stood
enamored of the great buck's
silhouette and held our fire.
But no, the thing was
dead and there was no beauty
about it anywhere.
 Not in grace
of movement (there was no movement)
nor in the velvet softness of brown eyes
(the eyes were filmed with death and flies
crawled on them).
 There was no hunger
for fresh meat, such as our own
ancestors knew. Fleas danced
on the hide and fat deer ticks
burst on our hands as we pulled the
thing to camp.
 The smell
was urine and wet hair. Blood
stained everything. We tied
the gutted carcass to our Jeep
and drove three hours to Challis.
 I wish I could say that love,
at least, survived those great times
that were never great. All that remains: antlers
rotting in some uncle's barn, the hide
too damaged to be kept; a picture
of strangers by a gutted buck.

## SAVING THE SNOWY OWL

Because I am old and will die
soon, I can surprise the young
petition bearers. *Oh, well,* I say,
*Without Owls, Mice Prosper!* The girl,
feather-soft and fragrant, shows
wide eyes to her helper,
who frowns and shuffles
leaflets. *Habitat,* she says.
He bobs his head.
*Species. Subspecies.*

*Do you cry at night for the dodo?*
I demand to know. My skin crinkles
and flakes. *Bring back,* I say, *the shaggy
mastodon!* But they are gone,
giggling along the walk an incantation
against lap robes and incontinence.

Others will sign the neatly numbered
pages, certain of change and time on endless
time to plan and do, while I
consider the plight of the snowy owl.
There is no saving us.

DROUGHT

We planted corn three times.
Wells went dry; we drank White River water.
Nobody drowned that summer.

There is a legend that some Indian god
demanded sacrifice and hid the clouds
until a dance was done and gifts were brought.

The Indians who were native to this land
are long since gone along a Trail of Tears,
taking their gods and totems.

We, victors and heirs, blue-eyed and fair,
base our living on a hybrid grain
derived from maize.

The year when rain was late and not enough,
we held three days of prayer
and paid our tithes.

## WHAT HAPPENS

What happens is that a thread
from your sweater gets caught
as you are making that quick dash
into Hudson's for a loaf of
bread and you go on, not knowing,
until there you are
without even a Maidenform.

What you want is to be ordinary,
almost invisible: a sand-colored brick
in a very long wall. You want
a house in Milpitas, a good Chevy
and nobody who remembers
standing behind you in the check-out line.

What you have is a line of thread
and your upbringing says you should
make it into something—
If only you had practical skills
like knitting or macrame.
It is always like this.

In your mind, you are running.
Be still. Be very still.
Think ecru.

## GREEN VALLEY, BROWN HILL

I brought a poem to my Creative Writing class.
It was about California and you. Mostly you. Someone
thought I should have said whether
the valley was planted with artichokes or soy beans,
was thin-green or blue-green, green as sea
water, green as the glass of soft drink bottles.

Some thought the poem should more clearly show
desire or antipathy, should explain why
I was still talking about you
after ten years.

I went back to the place where we had been and tried to remember
you standing by me, your hand on my ribcage—nothing erotic,
nothing particularly romantic. We stood at the roadside
market just south of San Jose, toward Gilroy, and commented
on the contrast of irrigated land, the dry mounds
of brown-hill California.

In my poem, I said that you had brought water to my desert place.
I called you my well driller, my great pump,
my maker of green valleys.
I might have called you my brown hill:
loving you, I learned things that were of no use to me.

Now there are houses instead of artichokes or soy beans
and you have married someone from Enid, Oklahoma—a place
    name from crossword puzzles.
The poem seems outdated and silly, yet there it is:
solid as a stock certificate or a last will and testament.

The valley was green: green as any valley.
Hill rose behind: brown hill.
At some point they joined, without fences.
This much is memory.

# MONDAY MORNING ON CAMPUS

Secretaries are the first
to come and turn the switches on.
Lights filter through a morning fog;
the coffee pots begin to groan.

Soon, early students straggle in,
awakening by slow degrees,
and three of them have read the text
and one of them has lost his keys.

The aging faculty are next
to limp along the ivied halls,
clutching their notes and copies of
the prints of Boucher and Chagall.

Above the snores and shufflings
they drone the words of Yeats and Freud
to pink-lipped girls and beardless men
whose minds are otherwise employed.

Another morning, other year,
the learners and the learned once more
come filing through the yellow fog
like moles along a tunnel floor.

## MY WORLD, MY FINGERHOLD, MY BYGOD APPLE

But Aunt Kate would have
taken a broom to it,
would have splashed pails of
soapsuds on the walls and cracks
of it, diced the apple,
put it on to steam with
    1 dash nutmeg
    1 pinch sugar
under a tight lid.

Uncle Raymond would have
leased the fingerhold
to a sharecropper,
sold the apple for
3.9 per hundredweight,
sent 3.9 cents to god
and gone riding off
to check the world's fences.

Out of a brown bag, I give
a wino my lunch, let him choose
whether to eat or sell
while I throw the world in the air,
curve my fingers to catch it,
maybe,
like an apple.

## EVERYWHERE I GO, I THINK OF YOU

White Oak Creek runs shallow over black grained
granite and flintstone. Below the spring it is all cold
sparkle and not deep enough to get ankles wet.
The banks are covered with purple
thistle and Queen Anne's lace that looks
pretty in spring, but turns to burrs
this time of year. There is no place to sit
and no place to swim and the spring would
take all day to fill a jug, at the rate it is flowing.

There was a time I thought that this
was one of the world's beautiful
places, with its pure spring
water and its granite bed, its banks
covered with wildflowers. There was a time
I thought that I would grow gracefully old
with you, loving and being loved, instead of finding,
at every failed stream, these metaphors.

## ON HIGHLAND STREET

It is 11:59 and the disk jockey on KHOZ
has cut Willie Nelson off in mid-twang to give us
news sponsored by Ace Hardware—
the latest from
    Bosnia,
    Sarajevo,
    Somalia—
war and famine and holocaust;
    New York,
    Los Angeles—
crime and poverty.

It is 11:59 on a southern July
morning on Highland Street. Dan Sears
walks from West Court to Circle Drive
and then from Circle Drive to West Court,
doing his doctor-recommended mile a day.
Martha Ledbetter tends her marigolds.
Across the street, Ann Graffy's son
is building a stick corral under the spruce tree.

I sit in my porch chair, sipping iced tea,
having done absolutely nothing to deserve
this fortune, this life.

HOW THE YOUNG LEARN
  (after watching a nature film on the Discovery Channel)

The people who shot the film are patient.
They come to this river each year to record
changes and patterns, to measure things,
to watch a silver-backed grizzly fish from the same rock,
one rear leg stretched unnaturally behind. They think
she might have an old injury, or a touch of arthritis, although
the stance does not look like something done for comfort.

And I don't think it is done intentionally to teach
the young cub anything. He is there
as my own children used to be always there—
on someone's hip, lap, shoulder, in the car's backseat,
standing behind me and pretending
to smoke cigarettes, drink whiskey, drive too fast.

The cub watches, practices from the safety of dry land.
He scoops gravels and tosses them over his shoulder.
As anyone might guess, he grows up. Silver-backed,
waddle-gaited, he walks into the camera's eye.
It is five years later. He mounts the rock,
swings his great body to and fro in search of proper
balance until, satisfied that he has done everything right,
he stretches his great hind leg back, awkwardly,
and stares into the river.

WOMAN AT THE BAR

In spite of Sunday
School prayers
twenty years ago
you will never walk
at night
without looking
over your shoulder
If you were my sister
I would offer you
my sweater
Loose women
in tight dresses
come
to a bad end
Ruby

It was the sins
of your father
brought you
here
of course
A Venus
you stepped
from his thigh
thirsty
needing a light

Your mother
was flat
between the legs
as a Barbie doll
When you
hunger
for the safety
of the womb
you lean
toward
any man
on the next stool

CLYTEMNESTRA:

How womanly patient, practical to make soup,
to re-adapt the country's laws to peace
after the army leaves to rape and kill
women and children on some other coast,
to mend draperies and update the plumbing, to mind
Orestes' education regardless of grief
he is destined to bring, being man and bound
by man's mandates. Grief is
your aging handmaid: useful, familiar.

How visionless of Aeschylus to suggest that
your chinless brother-in-law designed
a fitting welcome home, while you, unfit
and lacking wifely morals, fell
into treason and murder. Never mind
that Iphigenia was young

and kind and just beginning
to grow breasts. Her hair was soft;
it curled like wool around the ivory comb
you keep—you always keep—tucked in the bodice
of your regal gown. You say the right things,
private with grief.

And private with your anger,
once white-hot, now tempered to a blade
unbreakable, constant as fingernails.
How womanly wise you are to choose
the bath, where cleaning up is easy.

Fictional woman of the ancient world,
like you, I had a child who sang
the sun. First born. First dead. Her murderer
still wanders in the world,
feels sun and wind as if by right.

I clean the tub and mop the bathroom floor;
I dress and go to dinner, call on friends;
I think of you—more real than friends, sometimes;
but I do not forget.

# IN SEARCH OF AN ADDRESS

Ann says I am a snake in ecdysis, changing.
I will be, after the transition,
beautiful, Ann says, all solid
colors, having made up my mind to live
in this I am because I think I am . . .
     I think
that streets don't always
go like the map shows. Homestead
Boulevard cuts over half a block
and The Expressway isn't.
My children, in the back seat,
want to know if:
     1. we are lost, and
     2. we going to eat dinner.
More than anything, they want to know:
     3. Why divorce?
     4. What does their father say?
They are too young to read the map, to drive.
They can only remind me that we are passing
that same
     walking man,
     Texaco station,
     Church of the Good Shepherd
again.

DEAR DR. PEALE:

We're trying hard to follow your directions. We've heard the word
about this positive thinking. We would like to know what and, more
specifically, where you've been drinking; because something is being
added to our water and we're obsessed with genital inspection.

Whether it's with the opera crowd or on a talk show with a TV actress, or with
the Tuesday drunks at Wendy's Dew Drop Inn, at every gathering
we end up counting pubic hairs and measuring penises. (I seldom win.)
We worry about performance; there is no time for practice.

Norman, we admire you for your vision; but our rations have been laced
with hallucinogens. Could you tell us where to purchase manna?
People are waiting for the Great Celestial Saucer. On every hill from here
to Indiana, they have been talking to green-skinned Venusians.

It's like a modern version of pie in the sky, with everybody looking for salvation.
Some of us are hoarding and some of us are whoring; some of us
are trying to write a book that isn't boring, and some of us are
trading all our earthly goods for a reservation.

Dr. Peale, you seem to hold the answers, you seem to know exactly where
you're going. Do you have a map to truth inside your hat? We
blunder through a maze of plausibles around our artificial habitat.
Our stars are Trans-American and Boeing.

If you could help us fill the daily void with a new concept—not a variation,
merely, of God above with his mighty club, the devil below with a net
(That's part of our heritage, yet!), we would thank you for your assistance.
Most sincerely.

## FIRST CHOICE

*I am eating apples,*
she said.

He said,
*The moon's the*
*sun's reflection.*
*Earth is flat.*
*Who cares*
*which way we slide?*

*I do,*
she said
and took another bite.

UNCLE

They let us have
all our days but Sunday.
I was eight
and you had just come back from Normandy.

Grandpa said, "Don't
put that child on Bluebeard.
That crazy bronc ain't safe
for a man to ride!"

We left the barn at a slow,
jarring walk, riding the roan to where
hills screened us from view
and Bluebeard waited for his sugarcane.

That black horse had three gaits:
run, trot, and jump.
A Southern Baptist Hell
could not have held us.

My legs browned in the sun.
I tied my bonnet to the saddle horn and sang,
"Whoop a ti yi yo!" as we raced
right up the middle of Sugar Creek.

We rode across the bridge by Devore's house.
Bluebeard danced on his hind legs
half the way. And scared Mazel Devore
"almost to pieces," she told Grandpa later
when she looked up and saw me
"nigh to fallin', horse a rarin',
her just holdin' on . . ."

You married Kate that winter. When I came
in April—with the first forget-me-nots—
I sat on the gate and watched you hitch
Bluebeard to a plow.

*(Uncle)*

And I remember how the hills looked small,
As I walked home to help Kate with the dishes;
My taffeta petticoat and starched print dress
Making dull swish-swishes.

# THE PEOPLE I KEEP IN THEIR GREEN OLD HOUSE MOVE SLOW

The people I keep in their green old house move slow
when they move and their voices are dead
grass in December. They no longer hear each other.
How can we discuss possibility when I must cry
like a circus barker to be heard
and listen with a hand behind my ear?

Yet every word we've said before is
here, like dust under the old green rug,
*Stay with us.*
    *No.*
They follow me as I work, their canes tamp slow
rhythms of a dirge on floors that creak like fiddles
    out of tune
and as I wipe mold from a picture frame
they tell me about Lily—how she died
of gangrene and neglect in one of those homes
her own son put her in.
*Stay with us for what little time there is.*

They own the place where I was born. The road
no longer goes that way. That house is gone
and I don't know if wind or fire or time
sat on it until it fell
board by shingle into the underbrush.
This house is falling down.
I have spread tar on the roof,
built shelves for plates older than I will ever be.
It is no use—plaster drops into the pudding.
Yesterday I found a patch of moss
blooming in a corner of the washroom.

*Stay with us for what little time there is.*

Someone needs to stay and watch them die;
but I swear by the old green rug
and the old green chair and the green
old moss that grows on the slats of that goddam
old oak bucket that won't even hold water,
I swear I will not.
    No.

SPEAKING OF FEAR

*We have looked over our shoulders*
*until Dante wouldn't know what to do with us.*
*Alison, can't we just drink our tea—*
*perhaps with a little bourbon*
*when the wind sounds like a bagpipe in the juniper?*
*Must we lean on our elbows and stare?*
*There is no pattern in this residue;*
*tea leaves cling like tea leaves to the cup.*

I

I learned to swim where the creek turns.
We kept our clothes on, my sisters and I,
full skirts making our bodies heavy,
the water always cold and full of leaves;
snakes hung from hazelnut branches.

Mama says I should move my children here,
give them room to grow.
*Teach them of Jesus,* she says.
His head full of locust thorns.
His robe the color of polkberries.

• • •

The sign on Highway 7 says,
"Welcome to Boone County."
"Jesus will be coming soon," has been added
by the First Baptist Church of Harrison,
and underneath, a piece of cardboard:
"This frontage land for sale."

• • •

They came back—Mama, Papa—to the old house,
swept wasp nests from the parlor walls,
poisoned rats in the cellar;
left their grown children married and multiplying

on the San Francisco peninsula.
When I visit in August, I bring apricots and avocados.
I bring a dress to wear Sundays.
No one mentions my divorce
in the house where pictures of Jesus
sit among pictures of generations posed on every lawn.

• • •

Grandpa used to tell about a man
tried to run from a grass fire
and drowned
in White River.

Grandpa built the church
but never went inside. Built it
for the womenfolk
he said. He

sang off key
and changed the words
to Grandma's favorite hymns:
*Amazing snake how slick she crawl.*
*She'd bite a wretch like me.*

The bicycle chain
caught
as I was going down Marler Hill,
where red clay gets slick after rain,
and I went sliding on my belly
to a stop   nose

to blunt nose
with a copperhead.

Staring
I forgot
to scramble up   to grab
a rock   to say   yea
though I walk.

*(Speaking of Fear)*

Death has a tongue
like a witching stick.
Dry mouth.

White Oak Creek drifts
into pools where carp move to slow time.

The stone foundation of the old church
remains on this east bank.

I could build a house on these stones,
let vacation last forever,
never go back to San Francisco and its neon
kitetail of cities.

I could sell blackberries,
trap foxes.

A carp rises,
opening slow jaws—
there is something to close around.

There was a man from Corpus Christi, Texas,
caught rattlers
for a living;
braided their skins
into belts and bullwhips;
sold them in Tulsa
and Dallas
and Albuquerque.

● ● ●

On Marler Hill there was
a circle of red mud and copperhead
until that snake turned,
slid his cold tail across my hand.

II

Aunt Sylvia taught me how to fold pillowcases
in thirds, to place the forks
left side. She never married.

Our eyes were the same
blue.
*You could have been my little girl,*
she told me.

In the picture album: my blond curls
against my sister's
squaw braids; her
eyes, daddy's eyes,
black as thorn berries.

My thin face:
somebody else's child
brought in.

You couldn't tell Mama's hips from her waistline:
a solid Christian woman.
Her will
was God's will.
She couldn't stand the smell of alcohol,
but she could
wring a chicken's neck
without frowning.

Daddy, on his way to hell,
played guitar and hid
his White Mule
in the corn bin.

*(Speaking of Fear)*

• • •

*Jesus loves me, this I know*
*for the Bible tells me so.*
There were fifty-two
gold stars beside my name the year
that Dillard King took polio
and Pearl Whiteside got bit by a copperhead
down by Keener Trestle.

III

They bombed Pearl Harbor and we leased the farm
    to Uncle Clayton.
All the way to California I asked,
*Are we there?*

In San Francisco, when the sirens blew,
we turned lights off
and waited.
Night Wardens carried blue flashlights.
*Blackout! Blackout!*
Mama kneaded bread dough in the dark
whispering:
*In Jesusname. In Jesusname.*
Planes flew so low the windows rattled.

We are saved by grace.
Uncle Raymond came home from Normandy
with a disarmed hand grenade
made into a cigarette lighter.

Then every change of sky was earthquake weather.
Every night, The Lord was sure to come.
God told Mr. Kinsey in a dream
to move his family out of California.

● ● ●

I was given
more than I could use
and I was growing.

One by one,
I packed away
skirts that wouldn't button.

One night I sat on the window seat,
thumbed my nose at the first star.

*(Speaking of Fear)*

•••

Drive-in movies,
drive-in restaurants
in Tony Pucci's hand-waxed Mercury coupe—
furry carpet, custom-diamond-tuck upholstery,
liquid slick.
When we cruised Grand Avenue
even the college men would stare.

    like to have that baby
    like to ride
    be inside
    that cherry-body baby

In the first November rain, driving alone,
Tony wrapped that coupe around a bridge abutment.
I wanted to catch lightning bolts,
heave them back at the sky.

Instead, I went to church
three times a week,
read the entire Book of Revelations.

Tony lived and we
got drunk on his grandfather's wine
one Sunday morning
under Vine Street Bridge.

•••

It could have come like that, I guess:
the overhang of earth
boiling into the bay;
Hillside Boulevard split ten miles deep,
the mountain sliding.

64

Paradise Valley Church
could have floated free,
bobbed along like Noah's ark—
all God's children
keeping their feet dry.

$$\bullet\ \bullet\ \bullet$$

*Live by the sword and die,*
Reverend Blevins said when God
pulled both triggers of a double-barrel
on that moonshiner from Jasper.
*This train is bound for Glory.*
*Nobody ride but the righteous and the holy.*
We were up to Thursday of a seven day revival.

Remembering the night old Burton
Atkins fell on the church
steps and broke
his hip right after prayer meeting
and someone took the door
off its hinges to carry him: it is mixed
together like a box of snapshots
and postcards: the laying on
of hands, the pickup truck
tarpaulin stretched across cattle
racks, Doc Jensen answering
the door in his long
johns, Jack Roberts holding
Glennie Holsapple while she faints,
the church white
in moonlight,
its black
mouth open.

*(Speaking of Fear)*

IV

A dark Kentucky boy, driving a Lincoln,
took me for a ride.

He bought lobster,
champagne,
Trojans.

He bought a marriage license and Mama
called him *a fine boy, a fine boy.*
*His grandfather was first cousin to the Boones.*

*Marriage is forever,* Mama said.

I loved that Lincoln.
I loved his brushed suede jacket.
I loved the way my sister looked at him.

He said,
*Stay with me, Woman.*
It was something he had heard
Humphrey Bogart say to Kathryn Hepburn.

• • •

Our one-month anniversary, I woke
and left him sleeping.
I lay face down, in the park, and cried
until the sun brought children out to play.
But later, as I put the coffee on,
I smiled.

In twenty years of photographs: that smile—
above the heads of children,
at the zoo, holding the Christmas waffle iron.
That smile.
My back straight as a rifle barrel.

●●●

I wore the wedding ring until
it was no more than fine wire,
then took it off.
I put the cups away and swept the floor,
hung clean towels in the downstairs bath.
I gathered up the children
and we left.

*What was it like?* they asked old Ephram Roberts.
He'd been plowing on the ridge when a roar
*like forty freight trains*
plucked him where he stood.
He didn't even have a chance to yell
*Tornado!* 'til he was *sittin' by the spring, half-clothed,
watching that wind, yellow as a bruise,
rip through the sassafras.*

What was it like?
*'fore God, I don't know.
I didn't see the thing until it quit.*

*(Speaking of Fear)*

V

When my oldest daughter died, at eighteen,
I came to Mama's then. I walked
the old paths, some of them grown over
with young trees and some paved into highways.

Where Grandpa's barn once stood I found
his old milk stool and carried it down Marler Hill.
And on that curve
where red clay gets slick after rain
I stopped.

Death has a head
like a bullet's base,
dull eyes.

•••

My cousin said,
*Not everybody sees ghosts.*
*A ghost could stand on the courthouse steps;*
*maybe his mother would see him or somebody*
*who had wronged him once.*

Grandmother held me on her lap when I had chickenpox.
She sang Girls in Blue
over and over until I knew the words;
cut squares and triangles for my first quilt.
*That's just fine, Honey.*
*Now put the print next to the muslin*

She slept all day on Christmas.
New Year's Eve, we kept watch.
Mama fed her water in a spoon.

When she died, I slept
with my head under the quilts.
She could stand behind the closet door
all she wanted.

VI

You have to watch your feet in Boone County:
there are snakes.
And spiders, big as dinner plates, hide in the underbrush—
non-poisonous, they say, but nonetheless black, hairy.
Cottonmouth moccasins swim the creeks and rivers;
rattlers sun themselves on crossrail fences;
copperheads hide in berry patches;
scorpions, in this land of opportunity,
sleep in the closets full of patchwork quilts.

I have inherited a knowledge of Ozark seasons.
In April, wild grapes coil new growth
around the limbs of blackjacks; berries on the Old
Roark Place bloom as usual. Whether I
watch or not, the season's white and green
cover the bones of winter.

• • •

Donna arrived from Houston with her clothes
tied in a soup box, having given away
the luggage I bought for her birthday.
*I'm home!*

These children, portable as houseplants, leave,
they come back, they leave,
they come back to a rented apartment in California.
The young ones, still with me,
carry their roots in a suitcase.

In Boone County, Arkansas, seven generations of blood
kin: Edwards, Roark, Roberts, Patton,
wait the resurrection in White Oak Cemetery,
in that hard clay.

*(Speaking of Fear)*

• • •

Tonight, the gathering of the clan on Mama's porch:
Pearl and Elwin,
Earl and Evelyn Sue,
Elmo and Norma.
Someone will have to fetch Aunt
*Sylvia who has neither child nor man poor thing.*
I will sit on the old porch swing and listen
while banjos and guitars are tuned together.
*In the pines, in the pines, the sun never shines.*
*Lord, you shiver when the cold wind blow.*